Now and then

My history

Monica Hughes

Little Nippers

www.heinemann.co.uk/library
Visit our website to find out more information about **Heinemann Library** books.

To order:
☎ Phone 44 (0) 1865 888066
▤ Send a fax to 44 (0) 1865 314091
▢ Visit the Heinemann Bookshop at www.heinemann.co.uk/library to browse our catalogue and order online.

First published in Great Britain by Heinemann Library, Halley Court, Jordan Hill, Oxford OX2 8EJ, part of Harcourt Education.
Heinemann is a registered trademark of Harcourt Education Ltd.

© Harcourt Education Ltd 2003
The moral right of the proprietor has been asserted.

Editorial: Sarah Eason and Georga Godwin
Design: Jo Hinton-Malivoire and Tokay, Bicester, UK (www.tokay.co.uk)
Picture Research: Rosie Garai and Debra Weatherley
Production: Edward Moore

Originated by Dot Gradations Ltd
Printed and bound in China by South China Printing Company

ISBN 0 431 18644 8 (hardback)
07 06 05 04 03
10 9 8 7 6 5 4 3 2 1

ISBN 0 431 18649 9 (paperback)
07 06 05 04 03
10 9 8 7 6 5 4 3 2 1

British Library Cataloguing in Publication Data
Hughes, Monica
Now and Then – My History
306'.09
A full catalogue record for this book is available from the British Library.

Acknowledgements
The Publishers would like to thank the following for permission to reproduce photographs:
Alamy Images **pp. 5**, **14**, **19**; Bubbles/Andrew Compton **p. 16**; Bubbles/Fran Rombout **pp. 13**, **15**; Bubbles/Ian west **p. 12**; Bubbles/Jennie Woodcock **pp. 10**, **17**; Bubbles/Loisjoy Thurstun **pp. 11**, **21**; Corbis/Michael Neveux **p. 7**; Getty Images **p. 6**; Getty Images/Arthur Tilley **p. 20**; Getty Images/Daniel Pangbourne **p. 18**; Getty Images/Don Klumpp **p. 4**; Getty Images/Ty Allison **p. 8**; Masterfile/Ariel Skelley **p. 22**; Masterfile/George Contorakes **p. 23**; Photographers Library **p. 9**.

Cover photograph reproduced with permission of Masterfile/Kevin Dodge.

The Publishers would like to thank Annie Davy for her assistance in the preparation of this book.

Every effort has been made to contact copyright holders of any material reproduced in this book. Any omissions will be rectified in subsequent printings if notice is given to the Publishers.

Contents

Look how I have changed since I was a **little** baby.

Then

Clothes

My clothes are quite different now.

Then

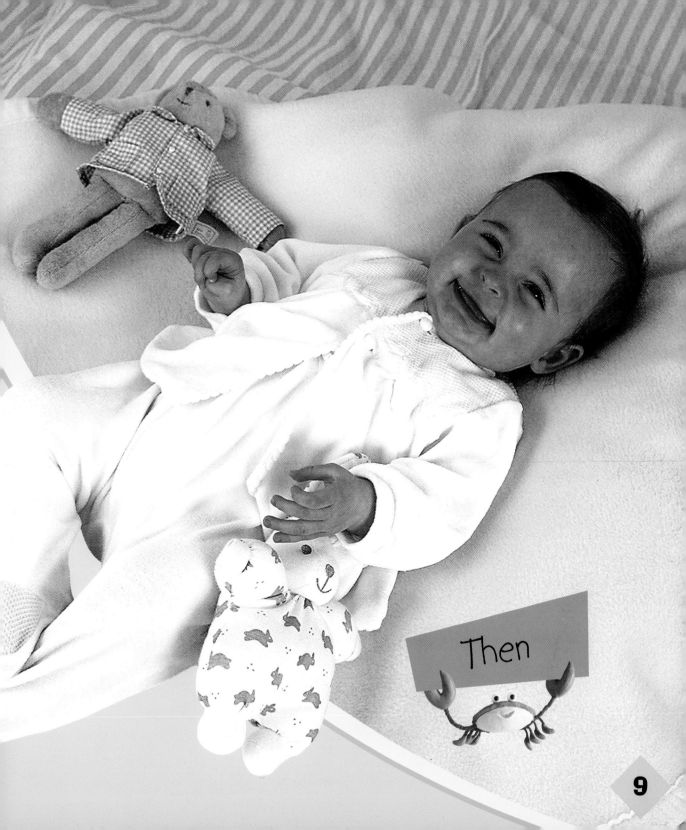

Then

Eating

Now

Using a knife and fork can be difficult.

A spoon was easy, but a bit **messy**!

Then

Sleeping in a bunk bed can be **fun**, but a cot was cosy.

Moving around

Now

Look how **fast** I can run!

14

This is me when I was learning to **crawl**.

Then

Out and about

Now

It's great riding bikes
in the park now.

A brick trolley was fun to push.

Then

Birthdays

Now birthday parties are quite **noisy** with all my friends.

Then

Once birthdays were very **quiet**.
Just Mum and Dad were there.

19

Holidays

Now

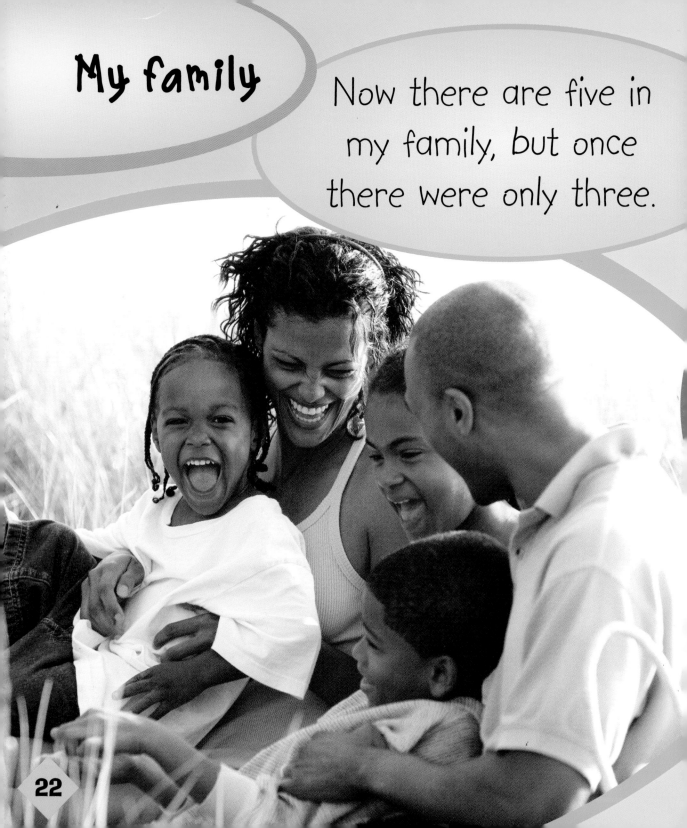

My family

Now there are five in my family, but once there were only three.

Index

The end

Notes for adults

This series supports the child's knowledge and understanding of their world, in particular their personal, social and emotional development. The following Early Learning Goals are relevant to the series:

• make connections between different parts of their life experience
• show an awareness of change
• begin to differentiate between past and present
• introduce language that enables them to talk about their experiences in greater depth and detail..

It is important to relate the **Now** photographs to the child's own experiences and so help them differentiate between their past and present. The **Then** photographs can be introduced by using phrases like: *When you were a baby, Before you could walk, When you were little, Before you went to school.* By comparing the two photographs they can begin to identify similarities and differences between the present and the past. Ask open-ended questions like: Do you remember when …? What was it like when …? How have you changed …? This will help the child to develop their own ideas and extend their thinking.

The child can reflect on its own past by recounting and reliving earlier experiences. They can identify ways in which they have changed, and describe aspects of themselves that haven't changed.

A follow up activity could involve the child making a record of its own past following a similar pattern to this book, selecting appropriate photographs. The labels **Now** & **Then** could be used help the child make a list of favourite toys, food, books etc.